you
health
at the **vdu**

a practical guide to reducing physical stress at the workplace

by Sheila Marks
Grad Dip Phys MCSP SRP Dip Nutrition
Chartered Physiotherapist

and Jean Oliver
Grad Dip Phys MCSP SRP MMACP
Chartered Physiotherapist

Illustrated by Martin Sandhill

European Business Foundation
Health Programme

Published 1996 in the UK by Health Monitoring Unit Limited

Disclaimer
Every position and exercise involves complex postural mechanisms which vary from person to person. The exercises set out in this booklet are helpful for most people most of the time. However, you may have a medical condition which needs specific treatment. If you experience any pain or discomfort, please consult your doctor, who can then diagnose your problem and advise you accordingly.

ISBN 0 9528060 0 2

contents

Foreword

EUROPEAN COMMISSION
DIRECTORATE GENERAL V
EMPLOYMENT, INDUSTRIAL RELATIONS AND SOCIAL AFFAIRS
Public health and safety at work
Occupational accidents and injuries

In today's increasingly competitive market-place, modern management tools and techniques are helping to ensure the continued success of businesses of all sizes. Increasingly, more reliance is being placed on video display units (VDUs) whose use in offices and in other places of work has rapidly increased. However, new techniques always bring with them attendant risks, which have to be evaluated.

In the case of VDUs, the European Community, in the late 1980s, considered that there was a need for new legislation to limit the risks for users of VDUs. Subsequently, on 29 May 1990, Council Directive 90/270/EEC was adopted on the minimum safety and health requirements for work with display screen equipment, which had to be transposed into national legislation by 31 December 1992.

Improvements in safety and health at work have also been shown to continue to a better economic performance in enterprises and undertakings. Whilst legislation lays down the basis for such improvements, it needs to be supplemented by appropriate information, education and training. This booklet, *Your health at the VDU*, is an invaluable aid to all those who have to use VDUs at their workplace. The authors are to be congratulated on putting together a booklet of this nature which provides guidance on how to use the VDUs and maintain a healthy workstyle.

Dr WJ Hunter
Director

Preface

European Business Foundation
Health Programme

360 million working days are lost annually in the UK through absenteeism, at a cost to industry of around £4 billion. To reduce this cost in both business and individual terms, the European Business Foundation has launched the Health Monitoring Programme which aims to:

- improve standards of employee health through preventive measures
- comply with legal requirements
- increase productivity and competitiveness
- reduce levels of avoidable stress and strain
- reduce the costs of absenteeism.

Most companies today are heavily dependent on their VDU operators, who are covered by European health and safety legal requirements. The first stage of the Programme comprises a computerised visual screening service in the workplace which assesses visual and physical stress. It provides reports and recommendations, identifying only those employees at risk.

This booklet has been written to increase awareness of the problems associated with VDU use and to provide practical solutions.

Anthony Frodsham CBE
Chairman of the European Business Foundation
Advisory Committee

Introduction – a healthy workstyle

People spend long periods of time sitting at their desk, without moving very much. To keep your body in one position your muscles have to work statically, which increases pressure inside them. Blood vessels become compressed. This reduces blood flow, causing a build-up of waste products, which results in muscle fatigue, discomfort and pain (Fig. 1).

Repetitive strain injury (RSI), now referred to as work-related upper limb disorder (WRULD) and other VDU-related symptoms, such as eyestrain, headache, neck- and backache, can be alleviated and avoided if you take appropriate action.

This booklet is designed to increase your awareness of body posture and to provide a practical approach to reducing physical stress by giving information on body mechanics, together with an exercise regime and advice on posture and lifting. It will help you to work more efficiently at the workstation.

Fig. 1   These postures lead to muscle fatigue.

Your spine

The spine is made up of a series of motion segments which consist of bones (vertebrae) connected by discs (Fig. 2). Looking at it from the side, you will see that it is curved; this gives it resilience and helps it to absorb stresses.

Each disc consists of an outer fibrous part (the annulus) and an inner gel (the nucleus). When weight is taken through the spine, the nucleus deforms and the annulus bulges like a car tyre, acting as a protective shock absorber. The discs also allow movement between the vertebrae: when we bend forwards or sit in a slouched position, the nuclei move backwards, (Figs. 3, 4); when we bend backwards the nuclei move forwards (Fig. 5). Since the back of the disc is weak, too much bending forwards stretches the outer fibres and displaces the nucleus backwards towards the spinal cord.

Behind the discs on each side are facet joints which help control the movements of the spine. Many ligaments connect the vertebrae to each other. These are cords of fibrous tissue which are highly sensitive to being stretched. If we bend forwards or slouch for long periods, our ligaments respond by becoming uncomfortable and then painful. This is a warning that further stretching will cause damage. In this way, the ligaments protect the structures underneath and also help to stabilise the vertebrae.

The spinal cord is a collection of nerves which are connected to the brain. These nerves emerge from the spinal cord at each motion segment through a canal and are distributed to different parts of the body. They activate the muscles but, when irritated, they cause pain.

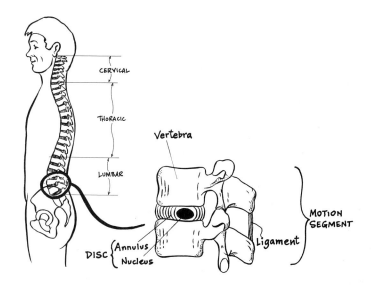

Fig. 2 The spine.

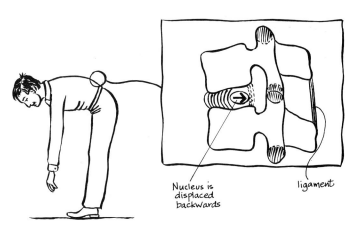

Fig. 3 The disc: bending forwards.

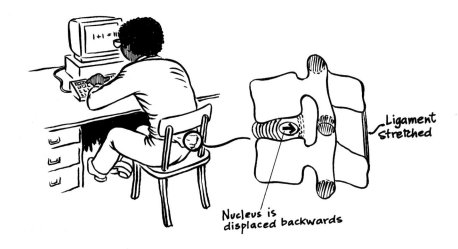

Ligament Stretched

Nucleus is displaced backwards

Fig. 4 Sitting slouched!

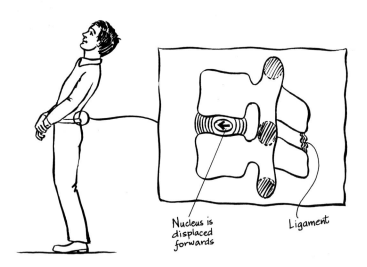

Nucleus is displaced forwards

Ligament

Fig. 5 The disc: bending backwards.

Your muscles

Muscles work in two ways: <u>statically</u> – to hold a particular posture, and <u>dynamically</u> – to produce movement.

<u>Static</u> muscle work is far less efficient than <u>dynamic</u> muscle work because it causes a build-up of pressure inside the muscles and lactic acid accumulates causing discomfort and fatigue. When the muscles work dynamically, however, contraction is followed by relaxation, which stimulates blood flow and disperses the lactic acid. Consequently, it is more tiring to hold a static posture than a moving one and it is, therefore, very important to do simple exercises periodically during the day to offset the detrimental effects of sitting still (see pp. 18-27).

In the same way as the muscles of the body become fatigued, the eye muscles, which allow the eyes to accommodate at different distances, become tense after fixed focusing for long periods of time. Whilst sitting in front of a VDU screen, the eyes are invariably focused at a distance of between 50cm and 70cm, and at an even shorter working distance when viewing hard copy if an adjoining document holder is not being used.

To relieve this tension it is best to look away from the screen for a few seconds every half-hour and to focus on something at least twenty metres away, preferably out of a window. Eye exercises are useful to counteract the effects of eye muscle tension, and they should be performed whilst sitting comfortably in a chair (see pp. 26-27).

Static muscle work is tiring!

Your hands and forearms

Tendons which attach the muscles in the forearms to the bones in the hands (Fig. 6) lie across the front and back of the wrists. When these muscles contract, they pull on the tendons and, consequently, move the fingers and wrists.

Problems can arise in the hands, wrists and forearms if they are used incorrectly. As far as possible, the hands should be used in line with the forearms (Fig. 7), with the wrists in a neutral position, i.e. not angled upwards, downwards or to one side. Using the hand repetitively at an angle to the forearm (Fig. 8) causes friction of the tendons in their protective sheaths, leading to inflammation, swelling and stiffness. Operating a keyboard or mouse also involves using the forearm muscles statically, which leads to a build-up of lactic acid in them. The resulting rise in pressure in the muscles causes fatigue and aching, and can also interfere with the function of adjacent nerves.

These problems can be prevented by maintaining good posture, using an ergonomically-designed workstation and regularly performing exercises (see pp. 18-25) to offset the effects of static muscle work. Using a wrist support can reduce muscle tension in the forearms and neck (Fig. 7).

If you use a mouse train yourself to operate it with your non-dominant hand as well as your dominant hand and alternate them during the day, e.g. two-hourly.

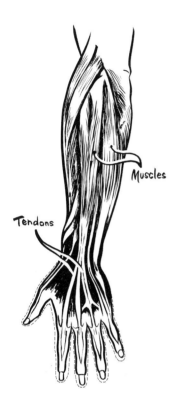

Fig. 7   Using a wrist support reduces muscle tension.

Fig. 6   The back of the forearm and hand.

Fig. 8   The wrist in a strained position.

Reducing physical stress

In order to achieve a healthy workstyle (Fig. 9), you will need to do the following:

1. Adjust your workstation to encourage good posture
    (see pp. 10-13).

2. Sit with a balanced posture
    (see pp. 14-15).

3. Relax and breathe correctly
    (see pp. 16-17).

4. Interrupt static postures throughout the day with movement and exercise breaks (see pp. 18-27).

5. Lift correctly
    (see pp. 28-31).

Fig. 9 A healthy workstyle.

Adjusting your workstation

Your chair

Start with the height of the seat. Adjust it so that the distance between the seat and the floor is the same as that between the crease behind your knee and the heel of your shoe. Your feet should rest comfortably on the floor – if they don't, use a footrest. If you are tall, pay particular attention to the height of your chair, as the standard chair height will usually be too low for you. There are specially designed chairs for taller people.

Next, the angle of the seat. Does it adjust so that it can slope forwards or backwards? If so, find the angle which helps you to sit with a balanced posture. Sloping the seat forwards will encourage you to straighten your back; sloping it backwards may make you slouch when you bend forwards over your desk. A posture wedge may be useful if the angle of your seat is not adjustable (Fig. 10).

The rake of the chair back. Is it more comfortable for you in a vertical position, or sloping slightly backwards? Adjust it to suit your back.

Is there adequate support in the area of your back where it is needed? Support in the hollow of the back suits some people; others prefer the support a bit lower, or even higher, behind the chest. If you need more support than your chair provides, add a backrest (Fig. 10).

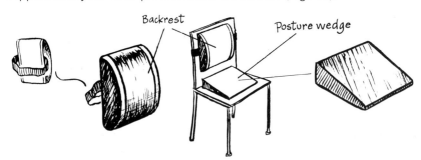

Fig. 10 Chair accessories.

Your desk

The relationship between the height of your chair and that of your desk is important. When using a keyboard or mouse, your upper arms should hang close to your body and your forearms should be horizontal, without you having to bend your back. Having adjusted your chair to the correct height, you may find that the desk is too high or too low. If it is too low, it can be raised by using blocks (Fig. 11); better still are height adjustable desks.

- If your chair has arms, they should not get in the way of your desk, otherwise you may find that you are sitting too far forward on your chair without adequate back support.

- It is important to have enough leg room underneath your desk for your legs to move freely.

Fig. 11 Desk blocks.

Your screen

- For comfortable viewing, when sitting with correct posture, the top of the screen or document holder should be placed at eye level so that when viewing the centre of the screen your eyes are depressed at an angle of about 15° (Fig. 12). Monitor risers can be used to raise your monitor (Fig. 13) or preferably, a swivel arm.

- If your back is stiff, you may prefer the monitor to be lower, as long as it does not encourage you to slouch forwards. Therefore, you will need to adjust your monitor accordingly.

- Arrange your screen so that lights are not reflected in it. Try not to sit directly facing a window, and prevent unwanted light with curtains or blinds. A quality screen filter can be used to reduce reflective glare.

- Remember that a clean screen is easier to view.

- However well designed your workstation is, sitting for long periods will inevitably cause some discomfort and you should therefore change your position at regular intervals. Standing for short periods while using your computer is beneficial, provided that you can adjust the height of your desk.

Fig. 12 A well-designed workstation. This set-up suits some people, but not everyone. Whatever you are looking at most of the time – be it screen or hard copy – should be directly in front of you so that you do not have to twist your body. It is important that you make adjustments to suit your body.

Fig. 13 Monitor risers.

Sitting with a balanced posture

Your aim should be to maintain the natural curves of your spine and not accentuate them:

- Having adjusted your chair to suit you (see p. 10), make sure that your feet are resting comfortably on the floor or footrest.

- First, sit so that your back is free of the backrest. Now round your low back (i.e. slouch) and then arch it (Fig. 14). Both of these extreme movements strain your back if held for too long (Figs. 15-16). In between these two extremes, find a position which feels comfortable and balanced. With your backrest suitably adjusted, let it now support you in this position (Fig. 17).

- Next, gently raise your rib cage just above your waist, and relax your shoulders downwards and backwards.

- Finally, tuck in your chin a little and lengthen your spine, as if you are being pulled upwards by the backs of the ears (or by your hair! Fig. 17).

- The correct posture may feel unusual at first, but it should not feel strained. Practise it every hour until it feels natural.

Fig. 14   Rounding and arching
the back.

Fig. 15 Rounded back. **Fig. 16** Arched back.

Fig. 17 Good posture! A straight back.

Breathing correctly

Breathing correctly should be completely natural to us, but some people tend to restrict their breathing to the top part of their lungs. Our lungs extend from the shoulder-blades to the waist. By using the lower part of them, we can increase our intake of oxygen and eliminate more carbon dioxide, which is a waste product. This type of breathing is called diaphragmatic breathing, the diaphragm being an important breathing muscle situated between the lower part of the lungs and the abdomen.

Certain factors interfere with diaphragmatic breathing, such as:

slouching – this prevents the air from getting to the lower part of the lungs and reduces chest expansion;

tension – (see p. 32) this tightens up the neck and shoulder muscles and causes shallow breathing. Excessive tension is not conducive to good health.

Deep breathing using your diaphragm

Stop for a moment and check that you are sitting comfortably in your chair, with your back supported. Loosen up your shoulders by circling them backwards a few times, and then let them relax. Now place one hand lightly on the front of your waist.

- Breathe in gently – your tummy should come out (Fig. 18).

- Breathe out slowly – your tummy should go in.

- Is this your natural breathing pattern, or is yours reversed?

- If you are breathing the wrong way, breathe out and allow your tummy to sink in effortlessly. Now let the air enter your lungs, filling them up like a bag so that your tummy comes out.

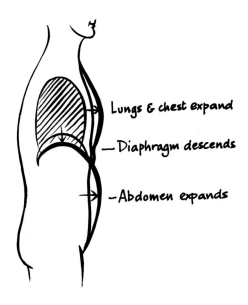

Lungs & chest expand

— Diaphragm descends

— Abdomen expands

Fig. 18 Breathing in.

- Repeat this three times at a comfortable speed.

- Remember to practise diaphragmatic breathing, and it will soon become a good habit.

Breathing correctly will also help to eliminate stagnant secretions in your lungs and will improve your general health. You should breathe correctly in all daily activities including walking, running and climbing stairs.

**Instead of taking the lift, walk up a flight of stairs
to your office, at least once a day,
practising diaphragmatic breathing at the same time.**

Exercise breaks

At the workstation, you should ideally take <u>mini breaks</u> at half-hourly intervals and <u>maxi breaks</u> at hourly intervals, especially towards the end of the working week to allay the build-up of stress. During each break, try to carry out as many exercises as possible, making sure that the complete programme is covered daily.

Mini break

Carry out each exercise three times at half-hourly intervals. Begin by moving forward in your chair. Take a few deep breaths (see p. 16), and correct your sitting posture (see p. 14).

1. Look away from the screen for a few seconds and focus your eyes on an object as far away as possible, preferably out of a window or along a corridor.

2. Circle your wrists first clockwise and then anti-clockwise (Fig. 19).

3. Tuck in your chin and lengthen your neck (Fig. 20). Relax.

4. Stretch your arms and wrists backwards with palms facing forwards and shoulders braced (Fig. 21). Relax.

<u>Return to your work with correct posture.</u>

**If any of these exercises causes pain,
seek professional advice.**

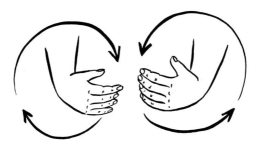

Fig. 19 Wrist circling.

Fig. 20 Chin in and lengthen your neck.

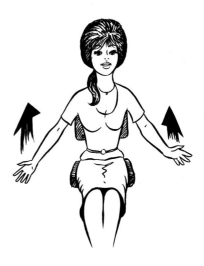

Fig. 21 Stretching your arms and wrists.

Maxi break

Carry out exercises 1-7 (Figs. 22-27) three times at hourly intervals. Begin by moving forward in your chair. Take a few deep breaths (see p.16), and correct your sitting posture (see pp. 14-15).

1. Tuck in your chin and lengthen your neck (see Fig. 20). Relax.

2. Turn your head slowly to look first over your right shoulder and then your left (Fig. 22).

3. Bend sideways, first to the right with your left arm stretched over your head; repeat the exercise to the left with your right arm stretched over your head (Fig. 23).

4. With your hands on your hips, gently rock your pelvis backwards and forwards so that you alternately round and arch your low back (Fig. 24).

**If any of these exercises causes pain,
seek professional advice.**

Fig. 22 Looking over your shoulder.

Fig. 23 Bending sideways.

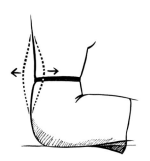

Fig. 24 Pelvic rocking.

5. With your elbows into your side, bend your wrists so that your palms face towards you and then away from you (Fig. 25).

6. In the same position, make a fist and then stretch out your fingers (Fig. 26).

7. Stand up with your legs comfortably apart and your hands on your hips. Looking straight ahead, push your hips forwards and lean backwards, bracing your shoulders (Fig. 27). Relax.

**If any of these exercises causes pain,
seek professional advice.**

Fig. 25 Wrist bends.

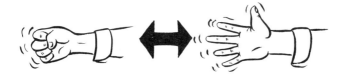

Fig. 26 Making a fist and stretching your fingers.

Fig. 27 Leaning backwards.

Remember!

Interrupt
static postures
with movement
and
exercise breaks

8. Now walk around your workstation before going back to work (Fig. 28).

Fig. 28 Walking around your workstation...AT A SLOWER PACE!

Eye Exercises

With your head as still and relaxed as possible, using minimum effort:

1. Move your eyes as far up and down as possible – six times, slowly and regularly. Repeat with a few seconds' rest in between (Fig. 29).

2. Move your eyes gently from side to side – six times. Repeat with a few seconds' rest in between (Fig. 30). You will find that the more relaxed the eye muscles become, the easier it will be to move your eyes further.

3. Hold up the index finger of your dominant hand (i.e. the hand with which you write) at about 20cm in front of your eyes. Keep your head still and focus first on your finger and then on any large object ten or more metres away, e.g. the door or a window. Look from one to the other six times, then rest for a few seconds. Repeat. Do this exercise fairly rapidly (Fig. 31).

If you suffer from eyestrain, you may need to visit an optometrist for an eye examination.

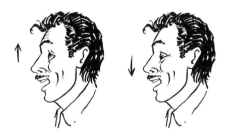

Fig. 29 Eyes moving up and down.

Fig. 30 Eyes moving from side to side.

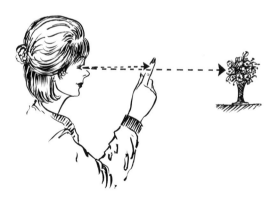

Fig. 31 Eyes focusing near and far.

Lifting correctly

Nearly a third of all industrial accidents are caused by incorrect lifting, so it is important to apply some general back safety principles.

Remember, prevention is better than cure!

Every time you lift a load, the pressure rises inside your discs. The pressure increases the heavier the load and also the further away from the body the load is lifted, due to extra leverage (Fig. 32). This is the most important principle to remember: Keep the load to be lifted close to the body (Fig. 33).

It is safer to lift loads which are between knee and shoulder height. Even if your knees are bent, it is difficult to lift objects from the floor without bending your back to some extent.

Wear suitable clothing when lifting – loose enough to allow you to move freely, but tight enough to avoid catching. Loose belts or loose sleeves can catch on objects and be dangerous. In some circumstances, gloves may be necessary to protect your hands from sharp objects. Wear suitable shoes to enable you to keep a firm, balanced stance.

Keep your workplace uncluttered to avoid having to lift at a distance, or tripping over objects.

Some people find that a lifter's belt, worn over their clothes (Fig. 33), is useful to support the low back when they have to do repetitive or heavy lifting.

Use mechanical aids whenever possible.

Fig. 32 Disc pressure increases with leverage.

Fig. 33 Stand close to the load.

Summary of principles for safe lifting

1. Think ahead: lift with your mind before you lift with your back!

   Are you wearing suitable clothing? Lifter's belt?
   Is the area cluttered?
   Is the load too heavy for you to lift on your own?
   If so, get help.

2. Stand close to the load (see Fig. 33).

3. Stand with your feet apart to give you a stable base.

4. If possible, face the direction in which you are going to move, to avoid twisting (Fig. 34).

5. Bend your knees and take a firm hold of the load.

6. Brace your tummy muscles to protect your back, or tighten your lifter's belt.

7. Lift smoothly without jerking.

8. Don't twist – move your feet instead.

9. The same principles apply when putting the object down.

10. Beware...Fig. 35!

KEEP CLOSE TO THE LOAD!

Fig. 34 Avoid twisting and face direction of movement.

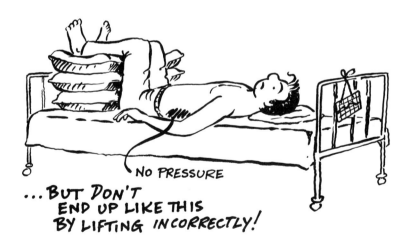

NO PRESSURE

...BUT DON'T END UP LIKE THIS BY LIFTING INCORRECTLY!

Fig. 35.

Psychological stress and muscular tension

Psychological stress is the reaction people have when they feel that excessive pressures are being placed upon them and they are unable to cope. It often produces muscular tension (Fig. 36). Do you recognise this?

Fortunately, not all stress is bad for you. 'Butterflies in the tummy' before an important meeting often has positive effects motivating you to give a really good performance. Many people in their daily lives thrive on difficult challenges, and without stress would simply lose motivation. However, more often than not, when stress threatens our security, status, beliefs and so on, our health takes a tumble. When such stress is prolonged, it can cause serious physical as well as mental problems.

You may find that some of the following factors* contribute to your feeling stressed:

- inadequate time to complete your job to your own and others' satisfaction

- lack of clear job definition

- no recognition for good job performance

- unco-operative or unsupportive superiors, co-workers or subordinates

- job insecurity

- no opportunity to utilise your personal talents or abilities effectively.

Fig. 36 Life can be difficult at times!

Understanding the cause of stress will help you to come to terms with it to some extent, but it is important to try to create an environment where there is co-operation and moral support between fellow workers.

You will find exercise beneficial in reducing both physical and emotional stress, <u>particularly walking</u>, as well as other relaxation techniques including deep breathing (see pp. 16-17), palming (see p. 34), yoga, and meditation.

*From 'Stress at work: does it concern you?' published by the European Foundation for the Improvement of Living and Working Conditions, 1994, with permission from the European Communities.

Palming

This is a useful method of relaxing, since it takes only a short time and can be easily incorporated into your work schedule.

Sit comfortably in a chair with your eyes gently closed (Fig. 37). Cover them with your palms slightly cupped and hands crossed, the left palm over the left eye and the right palm over the right eye, leaving your nose free. Do not exert any pressure on the eyes themselves.

Keeping your knees slightly apart, drop your elbows onto them or, if you prefer, rest your elbows on your desk. Relax and look into the blackness, imagining it growing blacker and blacker. Try to do this for a few minutes and repeat when necessary.

In order to relax as much as possible, it is advisable to deep breathe at the same time (see pp. 16-17).

Fig. 37 Palming.

**Whichever method of relaxation you choose, remember:
PREVENTION IS ALWAYS BETTER THAN CURE!**

<u>Notes</u>